40 Days Transforming Your Life

Naomi Sharp

Copyright © 2015 Naomi Sharp

All rights reserved. This book may not be reproduced in whole or in part without written permission from the author, except by a reviewer who may quote a brief passages in a review; not may any part of this book be reproduced, stored in a retrieval system, or transmitted in any form or by any means, electronic, mechanical, photocopying, recording or other, without written permission from the author.

ISBN-10: 1519227949

ISBN-13: 978-1519227942

DEDICATION

I dedicate this book to my wonderful friends who have joined me on this incredible journey. Supporting and celebrating many great moments and creating many memories of happiness.

CONTENTS

	Foreword	i
1	Introduction	1
2	Day One	11
3	Day Two	14
4	Day Three	17
5	Day Four	20
6	Day Five	24
7	Day Six	28
8	Day Seven	32
9	Day Eight	35
10	Day Nine	38
11	Day Ten	41
12	Day Eleven	44
13	Day Twelve	47
14	Day Thirteen	50
15	Day Fourteen	53

16	Day Fifteen	56
17	Day Sixteen	59
18	Day Seventeen	62
19	Day Eighteen	65
20	Day Nineteen	68
21	Day Twenty	71
22	Day Twenty- one	74
23	Day Twenty- two	77
24	Day Twenty- three	80
25	Day Twenty—four	83
26	Day Twenty- five	86
27	Day Twenty- six	89
28	Day Twenty- seven	92
29	Day Twenty- eight	95
30	Day Twenty- nine	98
31	Day Thirty	101
32	Day Thirty- one	104

33	Day Thirty-two	107
34	Day Thirty-three	110
35	Day Thirty-four	113
36	Day Thirty-five	116
37	Day Thirty-six	119
38	Day Thirty-seven	122
39	Day Thirty-eight	125
40	Day Thirty-nine	128
41	Day Forty	131
42	Conclusion	134
43	Other books by Naomi Sharp	141
44	About the author	144

FOREWORD

I bless this miracle inside of me

The day has come for me to set it free

I bless this miracle inside of me

I allow this miracle to soar high into the sky

And set down as a white feather by someone's side

I bless this miracle inside of me

I wish this miracle helps someone to see

All the love that is around them as it transforms

I bless this miracle inside of me

I let it go so it can heal someone else like it has healed me

Thank you God for helping me see

That all along, the miracle was me.

Naomi Sharp

1 INTRODUCTION

Many people talk about embarking on a life-changing journey or travelling around the world and having an adventure.

Well, by picking up and reading this book you have already made a commitment to embarking on that journey. It may have been instigated by an adversity that has happened or is currently happening in your life – that burning desire for the reality of life to look and be different. We focus on people around us and admire the qualities they have that we are seeking, whether that be beauty, confidence, love, ambition, a dream life style and so on.

For some of us we have what I like to call 'guardians' – those people who are present in our life who step in and help us. The friends who say 'this has got too out of hand', or the people you have never met that give you a gift for no other reason than to show that there are people around who care. This book is one of these guardians – to provide you with the opportunity for your life to transform.

This book offers you the information that you have been seeking–a way of starting the transformation ball rolling. To look at life in its simplest form, it consists of learning and transforming from one thing to the next; that's what we are here to do, evolve as mankind. To transform requires a need to acquire new knowledge and have a new perspective and understanding on life and, most of all, yourself.

The reason for this book is to help you to see that each day has a lesson and in that lesson a new part of you is revealed. Once it has been revealed then you have the opportunity to accept it and maybe even love that part of yourself. But here's the bonus: I am going to be here with you every step of the way offering signposts to help keep you moving forward. However, it is up to you how much you immerse yourself in the transformation, by knowing how much change in your life you are really desiring.

To begin with I want to share my definition of certain words so that we are both starting off from the same point:

Learning: making a whole bunch of mistakes until you reach the answer you are seeking.

Change: I liken dramatic change to being in a plane when you hit turbulence and suddenly drop a few feet. The majority of people's reactions aren't to jump for joy: the reaction is self-preservation as our survival instincts kick in. Gradual change (what the majority of us enjoy) is like setting out on a plane journey with the plane being one degree out on its flight path. You have a really lovely journey: the weather is beautiful, you have in-flight entertainment and food, yet when the plane touches down you are in a completely different destination, maybe you have even landed in paradise.

Day dreaming: I feel this is a good thing even though at school you were probably told off for daydreaming and not paying attention to the teacher. However, you need to rediscover the daydreaming part of yourself: the ability to lose yourself in a fantasy that brings you happiness, a brief period in time where you are free to create and live out the life you are dreaming of.

Last of all, transformation: imagine your day is like water running down a river and at some point you reach a pile of rocks (a symbol of the current obstacles) in your path. It takes a bit of effort to get over them but as you are pushing your way through you dislodge one of the rocks and it allows the river to flow a little quicker. As the river flows, the force knocks another rock out of your way and this continues to happen rock by rock, until you reach the tipping point where there is much more water flowing through. Then suddenly, numerous rocks fall out of the way and there is now nothing blocking the flow of water. It flows easily and effortlessly at a new level.

To begin with there are some decisions that need to be made. I have noticed, as I spend more time helping people, that there is one question I ask that always receives the same reaction: of people scratching their heads and looking puzzled. The same question is going to be asked of you; first of all you need to get a notebook, are you ready?

If I could guarantee that one wish would come true, what would you wish for?

In your notebook write down your answer. You don't have to be modest when you do this – you can dream big or small. It's all about you being able to make a choice, a decision about the destiny of your life. You don't need to rush when answering this question: take a moment or a whole day to decide upon your answer.

I am guessing by now that you have a healthy bit of scepticism developing. I bet you're thinking 'well, Naomi, that's all well and good but 1) I don't know HOW it's going to happen, and 2) have you seen my current reality?'.

Well, all I can say is that at this point along this journey together, I can't say how it's going to happen, when or even why. All I know is that by making that choice and allowing yourself to dream, you have opened yourself to begin seeing new opportunities and choices. For your life to change, it begins with changing a single thought.

Let's be more specific. By the end of the next 40 days what is it that you would like to have accomplished? Is it to receive a material possession, have new feelings about an activity or change the perception you have of yourself? It can be any one of these aspects or something similar. Write your answer down starting with 'In the next 40 days I hope to have accomplished'

The next thing to do is to look at your daily routine. How you spend your day currently is providing you with the life you have. It's important to note that when feeling low or even disempowered we are naturally defensive. When I speak of changing your routine I am not suggesting changing every aspect of your day. We all have different commitments and responsibilities. When I speak of changing your routine it's maybe 10 or 15 minutes in the morning and the same in the evening: a total of 20-30minutes per day.

This is when you may be tempted to say 'but I don't have time'. This is not a valid statement in my book: you do have time but you just don't recognise it, as your time is being allocated to things that you feel are a higher priority. I am here to say you and your happiness is the highest priority and you absolutely deserve 20-30 minutes a day of 'you time'. If you are finding the thought hard to comprehend, ask a friend or family member to ring you up each day for 10 minutes as you sit with a cup of tea and carry out your activities (which I will talk about in a minute).

Allow yourself this opportunity and after a few days you'll be surprised that you are still able to carry out everything you were before as well as fit in this new activity successfully. You may even have a bit more energy than usual as you have the chance each day to replenish yourself.

You have now decided what you want to achieve. You have COMMITTED to setting some time aside each day to an activity that will help you reach your goal or dream and for it to come true. Now is the time to decide what that activity is going to be.

When choosing your activity it needs to be something that doesn't seem a chore or too strenuous– it needs to be something that inspires you. There is no limit to the potential of what this activity can be. Here are some ideas to help fire up your imagination of what activity you can do:

- ♥ Write down and say 10 new thoughts, for example, 'I am beautiful, my heart is filled with happiness, I always have supportive people around me, my life is peaceful'.
- ♥ Have a picture that you love to look at that is a cue for your mind to start a daydream. You can live your dream and run through a day in your dream life.
- ♥ Create a PowerPoint presentation of pictures of all the things you are wanting. I suggest adding music as it always sparks emotions which help us to remember it better.
- ♥ Plan a walk that you could go on each day where you say thank you as if the thing you are wanting has already come true.
- ♥ Work with someone else: call them up or text them to share your new thoughts and ideas as if you are already living your goal or dream.
- ♥ There are some great videos (for example, guided meditation) on the internet so you may want to view one of these twice a day.

This list is by no means exhaustive and just contains a few ideas to get you started. Make it your own: it needs to be an activity that makes you feel good and that you are a happy to commit to carrying out for 40 days. Where does this fit into your routine? Well this is your choice and depends on what type of person you are and what lifestyle you have. For some people they will carry out the activity when they wake up in the morning and go to sleep at night, others will slot it in at some point during the day.

There is one last job to do before we take the first step on our journey together. On a calendar or diary I want you to mark 40 days. You might start today, tomorrow or even next week but choose a date and on each day write day 1, day 2, day 3and so on.

When I was marking these days I started to release just how long 40 days is. There is an idea that it takes 21 days for a habit to change. However, what I have discovered is that once you hit around 20-21 days, that's when you reach your extinction burst (I'll go into that in more detail later on in the book) where you cling on to your old thoughts, beliefs and values a bit tighter before you let them go. For some people they are able to let go and allow themselves to become what they are aspiring to be in 21 days. However, for others this is the point they may say 'I have just got to do this for one more day and then I can stop and go back to the way I was doing things before'.

When you then go for 40 days and you reach the 20 day point, you realise that you are only half way through, so you continue the activity and then by the time you reach day 35 you don't feel the need to give it up because it has become part of your life.

So go and find your diary or calendar and begin to mark days 1 to 40.

GROUND RULE – If you miss a day of carrying out your activity you MUST go back to day one and start again!

Now the reason this ground rule has been put in place is to reinforce your commitment to transforming. I have seen many people missing one day and thinking 'oh, I'll just do double tomorrow'. However, it doesn't work like that. Sometimes missing one day then turns into missing two, three or four days and then suddenly a week has gone by and nothing has been achieved towards your goals and dreams.

Now I appreciate that I can't check up on you as I may never meet you in person, but I trust you and trust that you will do what is best for yourself and your future. The healing, change and transformation comes from you, and I am happiest when people say it was themselves who changed their life around. I just provide the information that helps with the journey.

Check list

- [ ] You have written down (not just thought) what you would like to accomplish by the end of the 40 days.
- [ ] You have thought of an activity that you can do (preferably twice a day).
- [ ] You have marked out the 40 days on a calendar or in a diary.
- [ ] You understand and will follow the ground rule.

Let the fun of learning, changing, dreaming and transformation begin!

2 DAY ONE

Setting the goal of what you wish to achieve in 40 days

As part of the introduction you wrote down what dream or goal you want to achieve and created the new routine to attain it. Today you'll be feeling excited as you are no longer procrastinating over what should be or could be. You have changed your procrastination into action and, even better, inspired action!

It will be the first day you experience the thrill and rush of possibilities and opportunities. It may have crossed your mind what your life will be like in 39 days' time! It will hopefully look completely different! Let's explore that thought a bit further: how will your life look if the goal or dream you have set does come true? Would the way you speak and interact with other people be different? Will you spend your day differently?

Allow your imagination to fire up and go into a whirlwind of 'what ifs' and, most of all, allow yourself to dream. Spend your day living in a fantasy land, pretending you are that new person. You may get dressed up to go to the shops or arrange afternoon tea with your friends. Spend time allowing that childlike perspective to speak and play today.

You may have a sudden feeling of fear: it may only be a flicker but it is definitely present. This is normal as it's our safety default setting saying 'hang on a minute, if this comes true, look at all the things I will lose and what if I lose all those things and nothing replaces them, then where will I be?'.

Let's blow away this myth. It is a universal law (such as the law of gravity, law of masculine and feminine, law of polarity etc) of transmutation of energy or, in other words, we can't lose anything, it can only transform our life and thinking. It is up to us to find out what it has transformed into, and if we don't like what it has become then we just transform it again. Looking at it from this perspective there can't be any voids of where something is lost (I'm not talking about when we misplace our keys). I am talking about something no longer being a part of our life, and the arrival of unhappy feelings when we are so busy looking at where it once was and how it's no longer there instead of allowing ourselves to look at what it has transformed into, as it maybe one thing or lots of different things.

So today is about looking at the goal you have set, trying out your new routine, making sure it runs smoothly and dreaming. I would strongly suggest that, in your notebook, you jot down a few sentences about how you are feeling. Blow the cobwebs off your thesaurus and write down as many different positive words you can think of. These words will become part of your everyday vocabulary.

You'll need to have something to help you recall this day in a few weeks' time and remind you of how far you've come.

3 DAY TWO

The excitement of embarking on this journey

Today's theme is waking up in the morning and feeling really good and maybe even excited about the day ahead and all the possibilities. You may feel like bouncing around the house getting dressed in the morning or humming a tune as you take the children to school.

You will feel a new lease of life and you may even be feeling a bit more 'free'. Yesterday you had been given the key to unlock the ball and chain from around your ankle. All that effort and energy you were using to drag the ball and chain along can now be used to move forward in life. So, in essence, you were putting twice as much effort in and making less distance as you were dragging the ball of procrastination along and now you can use that same amount of energy and get twice as far.

Today what you need to do is bask, bask and bask! Basking in good feelings enables this to become your default setting and, most of all, don't feel guilty for being happy! When a person radiates happiness it has one of two effects on those around them: either it will lift them up and they then become happy too, or they get grumpy and move away from you or even try to make you unhappy because they are.

Stand your ground – you absolutely deserve happiness. Having the feeling of optimism doesn't mean that adversity doesn't occur. It will and that's when you will learn the most. But it means you can move through it a bit quicker and get back to your default setting of happiness.

> A happy life still contains adversity, but has the absence of worry.

It takes practice to be happy and it takes practise to be overwhelmed and any other emotions we have. What most people don't realise is that they have the choice and the confidence to allow themselves to feel and move around the variety of emotions they have been gifted with. I have seen some people in chronic pain and they are the life and soul of the party. Allow yourself to be the inspiration you are and by taking care of your happiness, it can help bring a smile to another person's face.

So as your day progresses, tell yourself well done for having the courage to demand life to change and for putting in place the ways it can. Congratulate yourself on letting go of your ball and chain of procrastination and allowing yourself to feel free, relief and maybe even excitement.

Take out your notebook and write how you're feeling and what happiness means to you. Praise yourself on what you have accomplished in one day. You have set a goal or dream, you have committed to it, you have done the first day of your new routine and you're feeling great. It's so important for you to practise seeing the small accomplishments you have made. Too many people look for the dramatic transformation in one day, however, most of us, like I explained in the introduction, don't like dramatic changes. But noticing all the little successes will help to keep you motivated over the next 40 days.

4 DAY THREE

Resisting the new routine and change

Well done, you have reached day three! Today brings an interesting experience of something that we go through on a daily basis, however, most of us don't even realise we are doing it – that is – resisting change.

Why do we resist something that we desire? It's not the dream we are resisting but rather the process. There is a lot of fear around change as it has been drilled into us from a young age to follow the crowd and stick with everyone else for life to be pain free. However, it is only pain free if the life you have is what you have dreamed of and want.

There is an old myth that we have to work hard to achieve our dreams – that we have to suffer our way there. No! Our day is made up of 24 hours and apart from the responsibilities that we have chosen to take on, the rest of the time is our own. We may use it to sleep, watch TV or read a book. You have already started to change the way you spend your time by changing your routine. Someone once said to me 'change your day and your life will change'.

It will take effort, persistence and, most of all, practise, but I say that you are worth that dedication and so are your dreams. Children have a brilliant way of being playful about experiences; this is an aspect I wish more adults would remember how to do because it sure does make the process a lot more fun. Learn to laugh at your mistakes, kiss your bumps and bruises better and go back to having fun.

One way of looking at resistance is thinking about trying to row upstream: it's possible but takes a lot of effort. As you row upstream against the current, life is trying to turn your boat around and take it in the opposite direction. Going with the current, you're screaming and getting angry, feeling tired, wondering why life won't help you along. (It is, by the way, it's saying turn your boat around.) Then you reach the extinction burst where you give it one last try with all your might. You get a bit further but you can't keep up this level of energy for long and you flop back into the boat lifting your arms up to the sky shouting 'why me!'.

As you lay there the boat starts to drift gently downstream, with no effort on your part it's carrying you along covering vast distances. You sit up, grab an oar and softly start to direct the boat so it doesn't hit the sides of the riverbank. You have the chance to enjoy the scenery, absorb the sunshine and then you see a building. You moor up and have a well-deserved cup of tea. That's what change should feel like, and trust me it takes practise to keep turning your boat around and going with the flow of life.

Let's look at how this happens in real life. The first scenario of going against the current is like us making our way through the day, grumbling how things aren't how they are meant to be and feeling helpless and frustrated. We put a lot of effort into thoughts that don't make us feel good and don't get us very far. The second scenario represents you flowing over the rapids in your day, enjoying the serenity of the still moments and having life work for you so you can achieve great things with little effort.

Today, as you walk around, feel the times when you're resistant to events, people around you, information or to the new routine as you practise it. Just imagine at these times that you are rowing upstream and then allow yourself to let go, the boat to turn around and go with the flow.

5 DAY FOUR

Emotional detoxing

Today you will be going through an emotional detox. No doubt you probably have lots of tasks to accomplish today. Your energy levels are low and the last thing you want to do is this new added activity as you feel you don't have time.

What is emotional detoxing? With a food detox there are one or two days when you feel rough or unwell as the body has started to receive the correct nutrients and hasn't received any new toxins in the last couple of days. The body is able to continue to cleanse as part of the process to optimum wellness. A lot of people feel lethargic because the body is working hard to dispel all the things it no longer needs and the built up toxins.

For the past few days you have been feeding your mind with dreams and wonderful thoughts, and now your mind is on a detox which also means your body will go on a detox too. So by just spending a few minutes every day on your new routine it is already having a profound effect on your own physical being, as the body readjusts to the new demands. You have also let go of some of your resistance to life, which means that your body has an opportunity to rest as the tension and stress leave your body. So don't worry if you wake up and feel like you have a cold coming on – it normally only lasts a day or so.

You may also find you enter the 'boxing ring' and have round one between your old beliefs and thoughts and the new ones you have chosen. This is going to happen a couple of times over the next 40 days. It is your safety default setting kicking in. All you need to do is allow those thoughts to surface and then, most importantly of all, let them go by reaffirming your new thoughts. It may feel like you are pretending but just stick with it. All will become clearer over the next few days.

This is a good time for you to acquire two new skills: the skill of letting go and the skill of dissolving worry. Everybody has their own way of letting go of something. It maybe writing a letter of all the things you want to say to someone or it maybe doing those tasks you promised you'd do for someone but never got round to it. For me, I work with a horse (who is acting as the metaphor of what I want to let go of) which follows me around the pen. I imagine there is an invisible cord between us and I cut it with a giant pair of scissors.

It may take a couple of attempts for you to find the best way to let go. In the end you will discover that it is a really worthwhile skill to have because there is going to be plenty more adversity in life for you to practise letting go of.

When I talk about letting go of something it's not that it won't be part of your story as it still will. It's just that it won't have any power or influence on your future decisions and choices.

Next, the skill of dissolving away worry. This is a simple task, however, sometimes the simplest things are the hardest to do. In your notebook write down your worries in one column and in a second column alongside each worry, write what skill you have today that could overcome that obstacle. You may also write down what skill you want to acquire to overcome a certain obstacle. For example, money is very often a worry. The skill you may want to employ is checking your bank balance daily and accepting that this is where you are at. The skill you may acquire is opening up a savings account and each week putting £1 into it. It's the new habits that transform life, not the amount.

Surrender your soul

Release your fears

Become whole once more

Playing and having fun

We hear your words

Even the ones that have not yet been spoken

We answer your prayers

As we make footprints in the sand together

We all have a pearl inside of us

Made from moments that asked us to be more

As we found peace in our pain

As we forgave those around us

So continue to live in light

And let that light grow

Surrender your soul

Release your fears

6 DAY FIVE

Receiving a curve ball

Whoosh, watch out! There goes another one of life's curve balls! Today you'll be experiencing adversity and one of life's curve balls. As the day progresses, you'll be asking yourself: 'do you really want life to transform? Are you absolutely sure you don't want to keep believing in your fears?'.

It may be that what you'd feared all along would happen if you embarked on the journey of changing your life. Or it may be that you receive another bill that needs to be paid to reiterate your current lack of money. Or someone saying nasty words to you, to continue to show that you are not worth it. Or it may just be your grocery bag splitting and all the food ending up on the floor.

I have noticed that only a handful of people move towards something because of a burning desire and ambition. Most of us move away from something because it is uncomfortable or we feel our back is up against the wall. That's how I want you to feel today: that things MUST change, that there is nothing left, that you are pinned up against that wall and you are going to explode and fight for yourself and your dreams.

That is the catalyst for a commitment to change and then, as you progress, you'll develop your goal/dream muscle and take action to change due to desire instead of desperation. When I talk about goals and dreams I don't mean targets that other people set for you to accomplish. The goal/dream muscle is your heart's longings: those experiences and daydreams that you have that you may even be scared to share with those around you. The more you practise setting your own goals and dreams (which is what you are experiencing over the 40 days) and doing something each day to accomplish them, you'll no longer wait for life to pin you against the wall. Instead you'll reach a goal or dream, then have a rest and enjoy your accomplishment, and then you'll be off again onto the next one.

However, I will say now that once your goal/dream muscle gets stronger you realise that the job never gets done. There is no need to get overwhelmed because some of the greatest transformational people who lived had a job list that extended beyond their own life and carried on after they died.

Here's something for you to think about over the course of today:

> As the junction looms
>
> The signpost pointing to the left says 'destination for the good life'
>
> The road looks smooth and consistent
>
> The signpost pointing to the right says 'destination for the great life'
>
> The road rises and falls, with pot holes and hidden pools of quick sand
>
> But the view when you reach the top is beyond words
>
> As you contemplate: what's the right direction?
>
> The first step is taken
>
> And you realise you could never take the wrong path
>
> Just not choose a path at all

Today I want to (metaphorically speaking) pick up your bat (of commitment and choice of path) and hit that curve ball back out into the cosmos, and know that you're going for the home run!

7 DAY SIX

Seeing your reality through honest eyes

Today is going to bring sadness and guilt. You've had five days feeling excited about your dreams and have had a few experiences of things beginning to change. But as we reach day 6 it's a day that we become present and see honestly where we are at in life.

It is a day that the veil is lifted and you see your current reality honestly, and a wave of sadness descends as you feel the contrast between where you want to be and where you currently are.

You may also be dipping into the feeling of guilt, remembering all the times you have dishonoured yourself, making promises to yourself and not sticking by them. There may have been times when you have not followed through with a certain choice or decision and then tried to please those around you and keep the peace or other people happy at the sacrifice of your own happiness.

Your task today is to accept all those decisions and choices: to let go of any guilt you feel for following your dreams, and find the confidence to say that two letter word 'no' to things that dishonour your morals, dreams or happiness.

Take out your notebook and write down all the ways that you feel you have let yourself down, all the broken promises you have made and not kept, all the dreams you had in the past but haven't fulfilled. Tears are good and, as we look at these things today, there might be quite a few. Let them flow, the phoenix's tears are healing and so are yours.

At the very end when you have run out of things to write, I would like you to conclude with this sentence 'I forgive myself for these decisions I have made in the past that didn't honour my dreams and happiness. I now let them go and their influence on any future decisions I make and I commit to honouring myself, feelings and dreams when making any future choices'.

Repeat this over and over again to yourself and allow yourself to feel empowered. You are ready to accept yourself for who you are, your strengths and those quirks that I like to call 'uniquenesses' that make us unique in the way we do things.

This is a great opportunity to share with you information regarding the emotional scale. We move up and down this scale every day as we have new experiences. The aim is to allow ourselves to move up and down this scale freely so the emotions we are feeling aren't hindering the progress being made in moving forward.

Here is the emotional scale, starting at the bottom:

Shame

Guilt

Apathy

Grief

Fear

Desire

Anger

Pride

Courage

Neutrality

Willingness

Acceptance

Reason

Love

Joy

Peace

From this you will be able to pinpoint where you are on the scale at this moment. This may change within the next five minutes. Having this baseline of truth of what you are feeling allows you to know what to look for to move up the scale. The aim is to be able to hover around the acceptance-love area, however, while you are letting go of some things today you may find yourself around the guilt area.

8 DAY SEVEN

The fire breathing dragon of anger is let out and takes flight

We have now moved up the emotional scale from guilt to anger. As the fire-breathing dragon of anger takes flights, all the frustration you feel is now allowed a chance to be seen and all those things that haven't been going right are told to hit the road and go away.

As you transform and no longer listen to people complaining, letting them pull you down the emotional scale or remembering the times you felt unsupported, they are all coming out into the light today.

For you to feel angry today is a good thing. It means you are moving up the emotional scale and not back down. It baffles me when people say when you're feeling low just feel joy. What they are asking is for you to go from the bottom of the scale right to the top all in one go. It's possible by those who have spent many years practising control over their thoughts, but for the rest of us who are either just starting on this journey or have only been on it for a few of years, we need to break it down into smaller steps.

Respect your anger but, like I mentioned for day 5, don't let it hinder your progress. Also know that your anger is not anyone else's problem so try not to 'let rip' on a loved one just because they didn't put a coaster under their cup of tea. Know that these feelings are because of your current perspective on life and on the choices you have made, and the tennis match between old and new beliefs in your head is at match point. Anger brings action and focus. Make sure today that you are focusing forward not backwards, be determined to reach the end of the 40 days and carry out your new routine each day.

Today you learn how to tame that dragon inside of you instead of it flying around breathing fire turning everything around you into ash. You let it take flight but in the direction of your new destination and for it to follow your orders and only burn things to ashes when you say and feel it's necessary.

Anger is not a bad emotion as it is the stepping stone from fear to courage (have another look at the emotional scale).It helps us to push off and leap up the emotional scale to find our courage to move past that which was making us feel afraid. However, untamed anger brings destruction to our lives. So, allow yourself to feel that dragon inside of you, allow it to be a part of you. With the experiences you have today use them as opportunities to tame and teach your dragon to be a help rather than a hindrance.

9 DAY EIGHT

Coming across new people, places and knowledge

Phew! You made it through the rapids! Now it's time to take stock and evaluate. It's a useful skill to be able to stop every now and then and check the map to see if you are still heading in the right direction.

How is your routine working? Is it feeling less of a chore to carry it out and has it begun to just be a part of your day? Today comes with a bucketful of relief as you let go and life continues to take you downstream.

There are certain coincidences that happen in life. I like to call them opportunities. They cross our path and can springboard us up to the next level, as you acquire new pieces of information and knowledge. It may come in the form of a book, article or conversation with another person and we can have the courage to take the opportunity it provides.

The piece of information may help you to see a new perspective on things, or it may provide a solution you have been seeking. However, it's not going to land on your lap and you clap your hands together saying 'right, job done, now what?' There needs to be a little effort on your part.

You need to remember the seeker inside of you: that place where captain curiosity lives and is joined by his crew of explorers. This is where you ask questions and those around you provide the answer. As adults we can become afraid to ask which results in missing the opportunities to have new experiences and learn new things.

But part of the reason you're embarking on this 40 day adventure is because you want something to change, and for something to change you need new information to provide you with the answers of what it is going to change into and how.

It's time to go web surfing!

Search around your topic area for blogs, articles, websites, videos and maybe pictures of people who have accomplished a goal/dream similar to yours.

Start to become comfortable being a part of this world. Allow yourself to see how people have accomplished the unthinkable. See how you are already a part of this new life that you want to achieve.

Taking out your notebook, jot down some of the things you have discovered such as useful websites, forums, a new person you have connected with or a picture of what you want life to look like.

They say knowledge is power, but first you have to be able to seek out that knowledge.

10 DAY NINE

Building the foundations

What makes up the foundation of you? It may seem a strange question and I bet some of you are replying cells, organs, blood etc.

What makes up your character? Your personality? Who is the person who is looking straight back at you in the mirror?

This is not the time to remove all the mirrors in the house, this is the time to stare right back at that person and own it. But the key here is to own the right part of you. Do you own your strengths or do you own your mistakes?

If you can imagine you have a bucket in your left hand and a bucket in your right hand. In you left hand the bucket contains your mistakes, weaknesses and imperfections (I don't think there is such a thing as an imperfection but some people do).For a lot of people the weakness bucket is never big enough, always full and at times overflowing. In your right hand is the bucket for your strengths, successes and achievements. Now I don't know who is manufacturing this bucket but there always seems to be a hole in it and when you look inside of it there are only a few things in the bottom, sometimes nothing at all.

Well here is a new strengths bucket (and without a hole I might add)!It is double the size and you need two hands to hold it. Throw away the old one and empty the weakness bucket onto the muck heap. By the end of the 40 days your strengths bucket will be overflowing with all your good qualities.

Here's the reason why:

'Your strengths are the foundation on which your dreams are built'

Just read that again:

'Your strengths are the foundation on which your dreams are built'

If you don't know what you are good at, then whatever future you try to build will come tumbling down the next time life shakes things up with adversity.

So in your notebook draw a big bucket that fills the page, and write in all your strengths, personal qualities and what other people may see in you that you don't just yet. Don't write in extra large letters to fill the bucket as you will be adding to it each day.

Sit back and look at your strengths, this is who is looking back at you in the mirror and by no means is this the full story. There are still lots of qualities yet to discover and life experiences will reveal these qualities to you piece by piece.

11 DAY TEN

Being more than you ever thought you could be

Today has such a wonderful gift for you. Today you are going to have a moment where you become that person who has received your goal or dream. You make a different choice that is more aligned with the 'new you' rather than the 'old you'.

In this moment in time you realise that you can be more than you ever thought you could be. You are well along the path to change and, for all the ups and downs over the last few days, today is the day that you see that small change occur.

It is so important to notice these small changes and recognise them for how great they are. Most of all, give yourself a huge pat on the back: one different choice here, another gift there and all these little things add up. When you take a step back you'll see the new picture of your life beginning to take shape.

In your notebook, on the page after your strengths bucket, head the page with 'Accomplishments' and list all the accomplishments, successes and achievements you have made so far. Remember to look at not only the big changes that have occurred but also the small ones.

This is a good time to look at risk. You have already taken a risk by changing your routine and I am sure over the last few days you have taken other risks too. Who knows, you may have even used that two letter word ('no') to someone. What is risk? Everyone likes to discuss and talk about taking a risk when thinking about a new life. The most common one is regarding quitting their job or giving up smoking. When you discuss the process that it entails with friends and family there are often heads nodding in agreement. But then you reach the end and they say 'as long as you can guarantee it will work'.

Ping! There it is. We will very often only take the risk if we can guarantee the end result is how we want it to be. Have a think about this. From your current place you can only see so far ahead of you as you stretch out of your comfort zone.

From this place if I guaranteed the end result you would probably happily begin your journey to accomplishing your goal or dream. Then you begin to make better progress than you first realised and you go above and beyond achieving things that you thought you would never be able to achieve, and you begin to see further ahead of you. Now would you still like that old guarantee or from this new place would you want the opportunity to change it to maybe something even greater?

Don't put a glass ceiling on yourself. Most people say others do that for us and that is true to an extent, but we have to believe that they have put it there for it to have an effect on us.

So, take the risk today to be yourself, and that means all those new things you are beginning to see in yourself that the new routine is revealing. Openly receive that gift, make that new choice or decision and know that it's down to you and the effort you have been putting in to changing.

> AND DON'T FORGET TO ADD TO YOUR STRENGTHS BUCKET TODAY (SEE, I DIDN'T FORGET!).

12 DAY ELEVEN

Standing face to face with your fears

> Northern star, shine your light
>
> On the darkest moments of my life
>
> Let your light be a beacon of hope
>
> As I make new footprints on this road
>
> Let your light guide me through
>
> To the place where my dreams come true

Boo! Do you see me lingering in the shadows? I am that one thought of fear that looms ready to stand in front of you, stopping you in your tracks, so you can't go any further.

You guessed it, today we will be addressing another fear that we have but, as you already know, we will be handling it in a completely different way. You are different now, when compared to the way you handled your fears six days ago, as you will be using the new knowledge that you have gained.

Take a look at this fear you're feeling or experiencing that is blocking you and stopping you from moving forward. Now take a look at the person you are becoming, look at the pages in your notebook of your strengths and the accomplishments that you have achieved (make sure you keep adding any new ones).

One aspect of the solution to your fear is that fear has no strength if you don't believe in it. The way we stop believing in it is to empower ourselves and we empower ourselves by recognising our virtues. We will all carryout something that we fear but, as you are beginning to realise, it is our choice if it disempowers or empowers us.

If you are feeling you are in a place of strength, take a step back and have a look at that fear. If you let this play out, how will it affect your decisions? What impact would that then have on your reality? And overall would that bring you closer to your goal or further away?

I believe that a part of your personality and character has the ability to move past that fear with courage and strength as you value yourself and your dreams. Instead of the fear controlling your decisions, you allow the empowered, wonderfully unique 'you' to make the choices.

I can appreciate that this maybe outside of your comfort zone and you may not be feeling confident, however, confidence is simply practising a specific action. You need to begin to practise and become confident in dedicating your thoughts to your aims and ambitions.

The more practice you have overcoming your fears, the more confident you become. The more confident you get the less fear you have and, if it does show up, it's not around for long.

The poem was written when I was on my day 11 and in it I choose not to look at the darkness around me but let that one star in the sky shine bright. That star is the symbol of my dream and represents me choosing to continue to follow it.

13 DAY TWELVE

Seeing some of your old reality play out

Today is a day of contrast but you no longer get involved, instead you just observe. There is a delay between when your thoughts and actions have changed to when they show up and become a part of your new reality. So, as you make your way through today you will be experiencing some of your old reality.

As the last little bits of your old reality play out, try not to get caught up in it and get frustrated that things aren't changing. Be an observer and know that you are making different choices now so your reality will be more consistently lined up with your new way of thinking and your goal or dream.

As you observe the day go by, it is a great opportunity to practise some gratitude. Say thank you to life and life's adversity for instigating and being a catalyst for this change, for coming across new information and knowledge on how to change, and for the courage and commitment you have shown over the last 12 days.

Many books speak of the power of gratitude and I think it is one of the most under utilised personal powers of all. Experience it for yourself, find things to say thank you for and allowing that stillness and peace to descend over your mind and body. Feel the relaxation as if you were lying on a deckchair on a warm summer's day.

This is a perfect time to touch on the subject of healing our past. If you think of a past experience that you have encountered such as a cut on your leg, there are two types of healing. The first one is to look at the wound, pick at it, poke it, maybe open it up and look a little deeper. Sometimes the wound will start to look a little worse. It's possible for the wound to heal, however, it will take longer and most likely leave a scar.

The second way (the one I enjoy working with) is to accept and acknowledge that you have a cut on your leg but, instead of picking it, leave it alone to let the body do its amazing work of healing. Concentrate on making sure the body has the right environment (nutrients, water, thoughts etc) to be able to carry out its wonderful work. If the whole body isn't on top form then the wound won't heal as quickly. What this looks like in real life is celebrating our uniqueness, seeing our strengths, feeling confident with making mistakes and learning, allowing us to love ourselves and being playful with life.

One day you'll look down at the wound and it has healed; you may have a mark but not a scar. The wound will always be a part of your story but won't affect you moving forward and making the most of life.

When you reach the end of the day, I want you to consciously take note of how you have shown such trust in life, in the process and most of all in yourself and your actions. That is something to truly celebrate and definitely worth adding to your accomplishments page!

14 DAY THIRTEEN

Choosing new over old

Thinking and living positively takes effort as you make a conscious decision to choose one thought over another. There was a great singer who once said 'I practise being happy every day'.

I think it is something worth spending time on and practising each day. This is what today is all about. Old thoughts may cross your mind during the day but you can banish them straight away. Right behind the old thoughts will be new thoughts that make you feel good. You can sit and contemplate, maybe repeat them a few times, because you are enjoying that feeling.

Let's look at one day's worth of thoughts. For every good thought you have, put a penny in a jar. For every thought lower down on the emotional scale, take a penny out. Imagine there is an infinite amount of pennies assigned to you. How much money do you think will be in your jar at the end of the day? Will you be a millionaire or in debt?

If this was a real situation and for every good thought you had you received a penny, I bet you would make more effort to think of good thoughts and you would be really quick to discard ones that don't line up with your goal or dream. You may even increase the amount of good thoughts you are thinking as you watch the jar getting fuller and fuller.

After a little while, depending on yourself-discipline, all the money you have saved up in that jar is all the money you need to obtain your dreams. You could stop working and get that other job, you could pay off your debts and mortgage, you could buy the dream car and so on.

What does this look like in reality? When you think good things you feel good and when you feel good you look good. When you look good you feel more confident and maybe do new things and meet new people. When you do new things and speak to new people you get different results. When you get different results you have a different reality.

And it all started with a single penny of happiness.

If this metaphor works for you, take extra notice of what you are thinking today. Maybe even mark in your notebook when you have a good thought, then scribble out one of your marks if you have a not so good thought. At the end of the day, tally up how many good thoughts you had, then try to beat it tomorrow.

Hint: this would be a great time to add some more things to your strengths bucket page and your successful accomplishments page.

15 DAY FOURTEEN

Clearing those things which you are procrastinating about

I hope you are feeling energetic today because we are going to be clearing all those things on your job list that you have never got round to doing. The act of procrastinating itself holds us back.

We have set our desires and, as we have spoken about before, there is a myth that all accomplishments should be a struggle, and if you receive it too easy then you don't deserve it. Well today we are getting rid of the hobbles; your mental worries are to be banished.

Pull out your notebook and write down all the things that you need to get done and all the things that you feel under pressure to complete such as answering emails, calling someone back or getting a present for someone. Whatever form procrastination has taken, write it all down.

Now put them in order, with the most important task for you to do first as number one and continue assigning a number to each job. Depending how much you have got planned for the day, start completing and ticking off the jobs starting at task number one. If you think of any other jobs then add them to the bottom of the job list. It may feel like a chore but you'll feel the benefits of delayed gratification soon.

It's important to recognise that each day brings its own jobs to do, and you'll receive new things to do everyday. The key is not to feel overwhelmed. See this as a great opportunity to recognise how valuable your time is.

The number one task on your job list is the most valuable way to spend your time right now. That is why you have chosen to put it as number one. It might not be something you enjoy or even want to do, but you have chosen it to be number one on your list because a part of you feels it is important. If someone else had the same list as you they may number the jobs differently because of what they value the most.

When people say they don't have time, they just don't value it as highly as some of the other things they have to do that day. So don't worry! You put that item on the list because you may have felt pressured to do it by someone else or because, by doing it, you believe you will feel happier.

Either way it is not there to bring you down or spend your happiness pennies, it is there to either take you closer to your goal/dream or give you more clarity on what you desire. But it only needs to hang around for as long as you want it to and, as I have mentioned before, your happiness and self-worth is of high value, so if it's not feeling good just get it over and done with and then you can move on.

By clearing this job list today, you have relieved yourself of the mental pressure and by doing that you will be turning your boat around and going with the flow of life. You have also created space for something new to arrive.

> You can't take hold of tomorrow's opportunities if you are still holding onto yesterday's experiences

16 DAY FIFTEEN

The truth about these 40 days

Today you will begin to see that things are starting to line up for you. By now you should have quite a few things on your strengths and accomplishments pages (add to them now if you haven't done so in the last few days). I am sure you have contemplated 'why is this working?'

Focus.

The 40 days is about bringing focus, allowing a portion of every single day to focus forward towards your future. We normally spend most of our day worrying about the past or the future 'what ifs'.

You have experienced 15 days of focusing on something that makes you feel good, that gets your cells tingling. You have given yourself permission to decide what it is you truly want, and have the self-belief to work towards it.

At these times I can't help but think of some of the greatest people who have lived, and they all practised the skill of focusing and each day working towards accomplishing their goals or dreams.

You are experiencing that working towards something doesn't mean that you have to dedicate 24 hours a day to it. You are able to work towards it and still live life as well.

It's an empowering place to be when you have completed this 40 days and achieved your goal or dream. Then you can start another set of 40 days and in one year you can have accomplished nine goals or dreams, nine things that you want to experience or receive. Think about new year resolutions where most people set a goal and then spend a year trying to achieve it but become unfocused halfway through the year and give up.

If you have set a really big dream you may have broken it down into little segments of 40 day blocks that all add up to accomplishing that goal or dream. For example, one set of 40 days may work on confidence, then self-love, then money, then career and finishing with family. You may then have reached that transformed life you were seeking.

Something that I have observed when people set out to achieve a goal or dream is that they line up their thoughts and have amazing imaginations but don't take any action. Either that or they take lots of action and stay really busy but don't have any direction or focus.

The skill you are practising is lining up thoughts with daily action, and hopefully as each day passes it will become a habit. It won't consume your life or impact drastically on your daily responsibilities but you still get time for you and your goal/dreams each day.

I would like to quickly touch on the concept of selfishness. It is not selfish to make sure that you have time each day to cater to your own needs and desires. It will make you feel more empowered and inspired when you are giving to others. I don't think being selfish is a bad thing if you're acting under this definition. It makes you feel better as you are able to absorb happiness from your dreams, and those around you are enjoying it because when you interact with them you're bubbling with enthusiasm which they can enjoy.

17 DAY SIXTEEN

Feeling change is on the way

When you wake up this morning I would like you to read your accomplishments page and notice all the small changes that have occurred. Now think back to the definition of change and how you wanted to be a degree out on your flight path.

With all these little changes you have achieved, where is your new destination? Is your new flight path going to take you and land on the island of your goal or dream? Are you going to go either side of it? I really hope you're not going in the opposite direction of the way you wanted to go. If so, during one of the last 16 days your plane has made a 'u' turn and is heading back to where it came from.

If you don't feel like you're on track with reaching your goal/dream, why is this? Don't become afraid and put the barriers down as you feel the need to protect yourself when I ask the question 'why?'. This is a problem solving exercise to discover an action you can take today which will enable you to be back on your flight path to reaching your goal/dream.

It may be the one thing you are most fearful of that needs to be done to be able to move forward. Take out your notebook and write down what it is you are fearful of, which one action feels like you will be taking on a furious dragon with a toothpick as your weapon.

You don't need to do anything else other than write it down as we will sort it out tomorrow.

Hopefully the act of acknowledging and accepting it means that you are feeling some relief. It won't have completely gone but will have helped you not to feel so overwhelmed by it.

As you move through the day just allow your mind to contemplate: 'if all these changes I am making do add up, then the probability of me accomplishing my goal/dream is getting greater as each day passes. Those changes have already occurred so there is no reason why it cannot continue to occur to the point of experiencing and living my goal/dream out in reality'.

Just imagine and feel the possibilities.

You are starting to discover and play around with the idea of change occurring because of a desire and not because of adversity. It is a wonderful experience as you choose to change your life because you are desiring something new, rather than being forced to change because of experiencing adversity.

18 DAY SEVENTEEN

Letting go

'I want things to change but I don't want to have to get rid of anything out of my current reality.' Imagine you are given a pebble to hold in your hand for every experience you have throughout the day. Towards the end of the day your hands will be getting full. The next day arrives and with it brings more pebbles of experiences, but this time of pebbles you really want.

What would you instinctively do? Drop the other pebbles and take the new pebble? So why is it that we find it so hard to let go of things in reality? It may be a past experience, material object or even a friendship or relationship.

Today you are going to let go of something and I suggest you look at a fear you wrote down yesterday. Today will be about letting go of that fear or something related to it.

Look back at how you let go of something on day four. Did that process work? Has the aspect you let go of no longer been influencing your decisions or actions? If it worked then repeat it with what you are wanting to let go of today. If it didn't fully work then alter it and try again.

It takes great courage to let go of something and follow your dreams but you have shown and demonstrated that courage for the past 16 days. Today is no different.

You have created space by letting go of one thing today. Instead of filling it with your goal/dream, I want you to allow that space to be a space filled with love for yourself. Life and the people around us make it very clear what our flaws are, or what is deemed to be a weakness, and what requires further work. We may be waiting a while for someone to give us compliments, and I am sure the ratio between receiving negative feedback to positive is leaning more towards the negative side. People love to criticise yet aren't very quick to compliment.

So don't wait for someone else to compliment you. Compliment yourself and remind yourself hourly what a great job you are doing. Start to explore loving yourself for who you are today.

There is no love compared to that of love for ourselves. Nothing a partner, boyfriend, family member or friend says can compare to that unconditional love that you have for yourself.

If jumping straight to love is too much of a leap, maybe try acceptance and work up to love on the emotional scale. During the day and every time you see yourself in a reflection or comment on an action you did or task you completed, make sure it is a loving comment such as 'I did a great job', 'well, that's another mistake under my belt but at least I have learned from it', 'I am radiating happiness today' or 'I look stunning today': play around with it.

By the end of the day, you should start to accept and even love that person who is staring back at you in the mirror. He or she is going to be your closest friend for life and, like any good friend, they love you no matter what you do or look like.

If you need some ideas of what is great about you read (and add) to your strengths and accomplishments page.

19 DAY EIGHTTEEN

Feeling free and basking in dream time

After all the work you have done over the last couple of days, clearing your job list and letting go, you deserve a well-earned break and reward for your efforts.

Today you will experience the feeling of freedom as you have freed your mind and body from fear and embellished it with hopes and dreams. Take a deep breath in and enjoy that freedom. Make sure you stop and acknowledge the feeling of being free.

While you're enjoying that feeling dip into visualising your future: how you imagine it to be, playing out scenarios of things going right, the endless ways of how the story might go, the people you meet or places you go. Allow yourself to daydream.

Today you will be feeling inspired and most probably inspiring others around you. With this new found feeling of inspiration, have a think: is there anything you would like to add to your routine?

Today you will receive what some call 'inspired action' and that is the golden type of action you can take, as it comes from your heart, from a place of joy. What you add to your routine could be absolutely anything: watching another video, making a vision board or creating a collage of inspiring photos.

Allow yourself to dream bigger than you ever thought you could, let an abundance of fun filled 'what ifs' arrive: what if I get that job, what if I meet Mr Right, what if I get that house.

As you are opening yourself up to receiving and allowing, there is truth behind the 'fake it till you make it' statement. It helps you to see and realise that the thing you are wanting begins with perceiving yourself differently.

Today is another great day to add more to your strengths and accomplishments page. As you sit on cloud nine, know that you absolutely deserve every great thing that happens today because of all the wonderful effort you have put in to deliberately creating this day.

Another great exercise to do on days like this(especially if you are less of a visual person)is to write a future journal entry. Write about your dream day as if it has happened today, filling the pages with fantastic experiences you had and actually receiving or reaching your goal or dream. Get down to the nitty gritty of the day including what may seem like small things but are monumental, for instance, waking up and feeling excited about the day ahead.

20 DAY NINETEEN

Rediscovering your passion for life

The good stuff just keeps on coming. Today is another great day!

As you go through the day your passion for life and what it holds grows. You may come across a video or photograph, or read someone's blog about a heart-warming experience.

Something will stir up that passion inside of you. That zest for life will flourish, go with it and let it run wild like untamed horses. It maybe something you never thought could be inspiring that gets your blood pumping. Feel the joy of no longer being held back by fear.

Rediscovering your passion for life brings an abundance of energy. The new thoughts may even inspire you to carryout some big action. Being around people who are passionate about something is so wonderful as you see them light up with joy, and you can't help but stop and listen to what they have to say. Passion is a great catalyst for change.

When we were children we role played, perhaps pretending to be batman or a princess, sharing our thoughts and gifts with others, suggesting and maybe sometimes demanding how things should go and play out. Yet as we move through our teenage years different factors affect us and the last thing we want to happen is to stand out. As people develop the ability to be invisible, to blend in, our desires, beliefs and values get put in a box in our minds and locked tightly away.

Every now and then we will come across something that makes us approach that box, we may even open it and have a peek inside but then we close it again and say 'I'll fulfil those dreams when I retire'.

Today go to that place in your mind where your dreams are stored, and open up the box and write down in your notebook all those things that get your heart beating, blood pumping, the thoughts and ideas of 'yes, I could make a big impact in this area', or places you have always wanted to visit.

Allow yourself to become passionate about something in life, it doesn't need to be sensible, realistic or even a part of your life right now, explore what would get you springing up out of bed every morning. It doesn't need to be the next celebrity, it maybe being a better wife/husband, daughter/son or helping at a community project.

Is it something you could add to your week? Even if it's just 30minutes or an hour. A group you could join or start, a place you could go to, or an activity you could carry out. You will begin to see that our time is worth spending on things that bring us passion and excitement.

Life is meant to be fun!

21 DAY TWENTY

No man's land

You are too far through this process and know too much to go back to the way things used to be. However, you are not yet close enough to be where you desire to be. You are in the middle of no man's land, a desolate place, a place where you may feel lost.

This is where you begin to realise the difference between want and need. You look back over the last 20 days with its ups and downs and reflect on how you were feeling, the trials and the accomplishments.

For some people who do a 21 day exercise to change their habits, they think 'I only have one more day to go and then I can return back to the way I was'. However, with the 40 day process you realise that you are only half way through your new routine and have the same amount of time to go through again.

This is one of the red flag days! Ensure you make time to carry out your routine because if you miss a day then you have to go back to day 1. You may be feeling lost and tired and this is why you made the notes in your notebook. Look back through them, look again at the reason why you chose the goal/dream, look at how things are already changing, how you have already made it through adversity and how it didn't stop you moving forward.

When we feel at our most lost we often look for a quick fix and instant gratification. What you are beginning to see is that in order to accomplish anything in life it takes focus, persistence and practice. On this day you will uncover your belief in yourself, your dreams and begin to trust in life.

That is not something that can be shown or taught: you need to discover it by yourself. Once you have discovered it, your belief will become a part of you no matter what life throws your way or what people say or do. That part of you is untouchable and will be your beacon of hope that you carry throughout life.

All you need is one successful experience of it working and then your belief grows. You will then seek another and another until you reach a point when you know undoubtedly that if you truly commit to something and keep focused, persisting and practising, what was once a dream will end up being a part of your reality.

This also goes for the not so good aspects: sometimes life does throw a curve ball of adversity and sometimes we create it because we are so focused on not wanting it to happen that we actually draw it upon ourselves by the choices and actions that we take.

By the end of today you will have reached a baseline of truth, about yourself and about life. This baseline is where you will spend the next 20 days building a different future. If there is one phrase to describe today it's 'discovering your integrity'.

22 DAY TWENTY ONE

Listening to your heart

After spending the day in no man's land you are one more step in the right direction to moving towards the thing you desire. Listen to the words you use today: Are you choosing different words? Are you speaking about life from a different perspective?

> If I am not good at it
>
> It doesn't make me weak
>
> I shall keep practising
>
> Until that part of me begins to shine with integrity
>
> And one day soon the world will celebrate what once made me unique.

The illusions that you have heard and believed in start to fall away and you may find yourself feeling anger and resentment about what you see. However, don't fall into the pit of judgement and criticism.

Everyone has a story to tell, about events that have affected them: the fact that they are still here and moving through another day takes courage. Think about the butterfly effect. If you truly want to change the world, begin by changing your day.

If you want to see more kindness, carry out an act of kindness. If you want to see more happiness, be part of an experience that helps someone to smile, and so on.

By carrying out these changes in your actions you are being a leader. You were born to lead through example which will then inspire another person to change their day through their actions. You will probably be asked how you do it. You can now share your story and experiences and the new choices you have made. You might provide another person with the missing piece to help them understand.

This person will then be an example to another person and so on until what was once a small ripple turns into a tidal wave. We just need to make sure the ripples we are creating are ones we want to see, of what we believe in and hopefully they will be for the greater good of mankind.

Move through the day doing things that bring you happiness. By this 'selfish' act you will then have more to give to others and will be an example of sharing joy and of turning things around.

Our actions can be good or bad but that is our choice, a choice we make everyday.

At the end of the day see if your choices are a reflection of how you want society to look. Many people have a lot of thoughts on how things should be yet don't do anything to change the one thing they do have control over: themselves, their actions and their thoughts. By acting with integrity and acting from your heart you will have a bigger effect on those around you – and much more so than you realise.

23 DAY TWENTY TWO

Seeing the new direction in which you are heading

As you go through today you are becoming more and more aware, not of life but of yourself. You know you are heading towards the destination you have chosen but the difficulty lies in the awareness of what you are leaving behind.

The old reality brought safety but not happiness. It is a concept that most of us decide to stick with because it makes us feel safe and it is not worth sacrificing to be happy. Yet you will begin to see the new part of you grow in strength and courage today, as your new thoughts and the beliefs you have been practising shine through.

You will make a conscious decision that your happiness is worth leaving the comfort and safety of the past behind. You will see the new direction clearer than you ever have before.

Take out your notebook and go to your strengths and accomplishments pages and add any new strengths you have uncovered over the last few days and any accomplishments you have made.

Look at the bucket full of your strengths and all those things you have accomplished, take note of all the stepping stones you have gone over that have taken you closer to where you want to go. Take pride and confidence in the fact that it was you who did it. It was you who took the steps forward, you made the different choice and you are allowing yourself to believe in your dreams and, most of all, yourself.

What an amazing accomplishment!

The accomplishment proves that it is worth walking away and leaving anything that no longer serves you –it should give you the strength to continue along this path. Where you seek comfort is beginning to change from those around you, or your environment, to you yourself.

Appreciate and write about what you are grateful about when heading in this new direction. What new opportunities have shown up that you didn't anticipate but have actually made the journey even better. To let go of something there needs to be something worth letting it go for, something you are excited to receive. It will help you to keep moving forward and persist with your routine.

I hope your routine is starting to become obsolete or maybe even a bit boring. That means the distance between you and your goal/dream is decreasing as it no longer feels out of reach or unattainable but you are just going through the motions to reach it.

Re-write what it is you want to achieve over these 40 days in your notebook to remind yourself of the direction you are heading in.

> Disappointments reaffirm the worth of a dream and the correctness of pursuing it every day.

24 DAY TWENTY THREE

Finding safety and comfort from within

I briefly touched on this yesterday, but we will go into it in more depth today. The feeling of finding safety and comfort is not necessarily from the people around you, your environment or even your material possessions. It comes from yourself, from your own thoughts and from that beacon of hope that your dreams will come true.

First we need to find out what it is that makes us feel safe. Is it knowing the bills will always be covered or that your children are ok? What things need to be in place for you to have nothing to worry about so you can be the person you always wanted to be?

Take out your notebook and write down the answer to the question: What do I need to feel safe?

It doesn't matter how long the list is and you may even fill up the rest of your notebook with the answer. Take a look at your answers: Why do those things make you feel safe? Is it because it's a place to hide or become invisible? Is it because by having that material possession you feel protected from society?

Hopefully you are beginning to see that safety and comfort are simply perceptions, beliefs that they will shield you from anything bad happening. I guess at some point in your life you have experienced that one thing that you believed would save you and didn't do it and your worse fears came true. Did you survive? It may have left a few scars behind.

Today is about strengthening your trust in yourself. We looked at this a few days ago but, as you know, part of this 40 day process is practice.

Find experiences today that push you out of your comfort zone, that stretch you a little and can help strengthen your belief in yourself and your ability. Trust in yourself and the reasons why you need to accomplish your dream or goal.

Start to trust in your own opinion and allow it to be heard. Start to see that those things that you thought made you feel safe have helped reflect your ability to feel safe by trusting your own judgement.

We can learn to look for safety and comfort from within, to know that we can turn our thoughts around and see a single flower in a vast desert. You have started to free yourself and with that freedom you lose the fear that was holding you back from trying new things or making mistakes.

Today has the potential to be a springboard, sending you further along your path, quicker and with little effort needed. You will then have experienced what I call 'quantum leaping', as you take that one action that you were afraid to do but you did it anyway and it flings you forward closer to your goal or dream.

25 DAY TWENTY FOUR

Seeing the higher purpose of your actions and dreams

As we move through life and its different experiences it provides us with opportunities to give to others but also to society as a whole. By what you experience, even the most traumatic things a human can go through can then be a catalyst for change amongst mankind.

So today is about uncovering the greatness in you.

When I talk about greatness is doesn't mean that the only people who have displayed greatness is those who have invented something or been inspiring public speakers.

Greatness is in your actions. Being yourself and allowing your inner truth to shine has an impact on the way society functions. There are many unsung heroes in society: carers, people who are optimistic even though they have been through traumatic experiences, medical miracles and the waste collectors who help to keep our streets clean.

It's about recognising the small acts of greatness that people do everyday. This includes you. Don't wait for society to give you a big award. Know yourself what a difference you are making to those around you.

If you can't seem to recognise or see an act of greatness that you have carried out recently, make sure you see one today. For example, letting someone pull out of a junction may have been of greater help to that person than you realise.

That person may have been in a hurry to get to the hospital to see a relative or their child, or they may have been going for a job interview for their dream job. A smile you gave someone as they entered the shop may have helped cheer them up as it made them feel recognised and no longer invisible. That smile gave someone hope and they may then pass it on to another person as they get on the bus.

As we move through our day we are sometimes unaware of people around us and sometimes afraid to ask what it is they are striving for. Is that day just another day for them or is it a day that something wonderful or terrifying is going to happen? Listen and also share your dreams with the people around you and you'll be surprised. A person sitting opposite you in the coffee shop may be the person with the solution or who can provide the opportunity for your dreams to come true.

Take out your notebook and draw a heart or a symbol you would like to use for greatness and, just like your strengths bucket page, write down the acts of greatness that you have carried out. It doesn't matter how long ago or how small they may seem. It may even be your thoroughness in washing the pots after a meal or the way you make the best cup of tea. Write them all down.

Allow yourself to see the greatness you have within you that you may never have allowed yourself to see for fear of being arrogant. Greatness is enabling your inner truths to be of service and help to those you meet.

26 DAY TWENTY FIVE

Recognising an opportunity

Every day provides many opportunities and most of us think of opportunities as our jobs list. They are indeed opportunities yet most people associate a jobs list with stress, worry and pressure. Because of this they may not take full advantage of the opportunities.

Sometimes we think of opportunities as making it through the auditions on a talent show, however, this would be a dramatic change and not many people voluntarily choose that.

Look at the day you have planned out: What opportunities does it have? What opportunities do you want it to have? Do you want to receive the call from a long lost relative and begin rebuilding family connections, or the opportunity to start receiving more money?

Are you beginning to see the key to unlock the door? We have many opportunities for many different experiences and you just need to know which opportunity you are seeking. The opportunity to take you to the next step may present itself everyday, however, if you're not looking for it then it will probably pass you by.

Let's say you have decided the area of life in which you are looking for an opportunity to occur (I am presuming it will be something to do with your goal/dream) and a coincidence happens during that day and you recognise it as an opportunity. Are you going to just stand and look at it or are you going to reach out and take it?

How many times have you heard yourself say 'if this happens I am definitely going to tell them how I feel, or share my ideas or act more confidently'? How many times has that situation arrived and when it came to it you just froze or couldn't find your voice.

It takes confidence to take hold of an opportunity. Confidence is simply practising a specific action. Think of someone doing something confidently – how many times or hours do you think they have practised that action? I would predict that it would be in the thousands.

Repetition, repetition, repetition.

There is no shortcut–all that is needed is dedication. Hopefully you're inspired enough to keep going, even on the days when you want to pull the duvet up over your head and groan about getting out of bed a little earlier to get carry out your new routine.

The more you practise taking an opportunity, the more confident you'll get and the more confident you get the faster you will accomplish your goals/ dreams. As I have said before, don't worry if you take a few opportunities and they don't quite work out as you planned. My definition of learning is making a whole bunch of mistakes until you reach the answer you are looking for. So just look for the next opportunity to continue to move forward.

This is quite fun to do with a friend. Share what opportunity you are looking for (and your friend may want to do the same), and then when the opportunity arrives they can help to make sure you take it.

> It's not when or even if the opportunity will arrive, it's will we have the courage to take it when it does arrive.

27 DAY TWENTY SIX

Your dream will definitely come true

Today is a research day as you build on what you uncovered on day 8. You will definitely be needing your notebook today! The goal/dream you set on day 1 was set because it inspired you and gave you a bubble of excitement of having the potential to bring you more happiness.

Today shouldn't be a laborious task. If anything, by the end of the day you should be bouncing off the walls with excitement. As you explore the area of your goal/dream further, go to the library for some books or take a look at the internet.

Watch and read how other people have achieved similar things and learn from their journey. See what steps they took, what actions they carried out, even who they contacted.

By the end of this day you are going to be an expert. You may receive a clue about what you should do next and take that opportunity. As you probably know, research is about understanding a topic further. You can go as deep as you want to.

The more you know, the more you will see and the more connections will begin to be made to your life. It's also important for you to recognise that, by your actions today, you are being very committed to the goal/dream you have set.

That is very admiral!

Have you also noticed that when you speak to other people about accomplishing your goal/dream that they no longer look at you as if you are in cuckoo land. They too are believing in your dreams and may even take interest in how you are accomplishing them so well.

Take pride in that and write it in your strengths bucket. You have the belief in yourself to know that, even though it can't be seen just yet, it will become a physical experience. Feel free to add any more aspects to your strengths and accomplishments pages.

How is your notebook looking? Have you uncovered something new or come across some information that reminded you that you haven't completed a task yet? Let today build on yesterday's accomplishments and take action on that opportunity, keep practising and allowing your greatness to shine.

Another red flag moment! To ensure that you continue to carry out your routine, don't let yourself become overwhelmed today as you research your area. There will be a lot of information available to you, trust your gut feeling on things, if it's not making sense then try another source.

If you are starting to build a monumental task list, then limit yourself to six tasks and once you have completed those six tasks then you can add your next six tasks to the list. By the time you finish those first six tasks some of the other ones may then become obsolete.

28 DAY TWENTY SEVEN

Acting on courage

You have reached day 27 and you may be feeling a lot of frustration today. You have continued with the routine for the past 20 days and another week has gone by and you may be wondering what you have got to show for it. You have yet to stand in the moment where your goal/dream is a reality.

Over the past few days you have discovered the courage to take opportunities. Look back to the emotional scale on day 6 where you were hovering around the level of fear. You then went through anger and for the last few days you have been sitting around the level of courage.

Today it's time to take the next leap up the emotional scale to acceptance. What is meant by acceptance? It doesn't mean settling; there is a definite difference. Acceptance is knowing where you are but also knowing that you are still moving forward; settling is knowing where you are and feeling powerless to change it.

Recognise that you have another 13 days to go which is just under two weeks. Flick through your notebook and look how much you have achieved over the last two weeks. Imagine where you'll be or the place you are going to reach with that same amount of time again and with your new knowledge and skills. I'm sure you'll surprise yourself.

There is an age-old saying 'enjoy the journey'. There is a lot of truth in this statement and it is a good skill to master. To begin to do it you must start by accepting the place you are at in this moment.

When people are healing and find acceptance in who they are in that moment – all of themselves including the good stuff and the things they are wanting to improve– they relieve themselves of a burden and any pressure that was created.

Once they are able to relax and take a 'bugger it' pill they then move into a place of allowing, and a lot of what they were trying to hide doesn't show up because they aren't putting all their effort and energy into stopping it. So it loses its power and they are able to direct that energy to something they do want to grow.

So today, give yourself some TLC. Do something that makes you feel happy or put on a movie and get lost in a love story, or watch a comedy and let the tears be from laughter rather than desperation.

Align your thoughts with 'it's fine to be where I am today because tomorrow is going to arrive and I am going to be in a different place and by the end of the day I will be one day closer to reaching my goal or dream.' Re-read your accomplishments page and allow it to be your motivation. You have achieved all those things in 27 days and you can achieve the same amount or even more again over the next couple of weeks.

29 DAY TWENTY EIGHT

Why we say thank you

Now we will be building on what we have already learned about gratitude. When we say thank you for something it normally means that we have received it and we like what we have received. So why is it that we don't usually say thank you for the small occurrences that have happened leading up to the grand prize.

Sometimes we become so focused on the end goal that we forget to recognise all those little stepping stones we have walked over to get there. You can now build on what you were practising yesterday: enjoying the journey and accepting where you are at this moment in time.

I want you to continue to explore being thankful and spending a moment in gratitude for all those coincidences, tears and gifts that you have received so far. Hopefully you can go one step closer and start to look at all those wonderful things that are waiting for you to receive in the future.

If you look at what you want in the future and start from a place where you are already saying thank you for it, you are reaffirming to yourself that you are already well on your way to receiving it. You are not staring at the empty space in your life and where you want it to go, and feeling its absence as it is not a part of your life. The latter thoughts can quickly send you on a slide down the emotional scale to apathy where you lose all enthusiasm in your goal or dream.

Let's look at an example. Imagine you are walking down the high street and walk past a jewellery store. You see a beautiful necklace and earring set and for a man you see a stunning watch. You stare at it and get a rush of desire: you know the perfect occasion you could wear it for.

Your imagination fires up as you see yourself putting it on and looking at it in the mirror as it makes you feel wonderful. Then you continue to carry on walking down the street, knowing that you are not quite ready to buy it or spend that amount of money today. But instead of feeling disappointment you can say thank you: to the jeweller who designed it, to the people who carefully crafted and created it, to the shop for seeing its beauty and displaying it in the front window, to yourself for choosing that street to walk down.

By saying thank you, you aren't denying yourself any of those happy feelings that the item gives you. If anything, you are receiving all those good feelings before you have even purchased anything. It is why you desired it in the first place –to experience the good feelings.

So exploring your gratitude for something doesn't mean that you say thank you and 'ping!' it arrives. It's about allowing yourself worth to flourish again and to feel those good feelings even before you have received it because you deserve that happiness in this moment.

And, who knows? The next time you walk past the shop window they may have it on sale at a price you feel more comfortable with and you can seize that opportunity.

30 DAY TWENTY NINE

Bang! There goes the extinction burst

For those around you it may be a day to take cover as the fire breathing dragon from the deep, dark depths of your mind comes raging out to fight to save those final few thoughts and beliefs that no longer serve you.

Today you are going to experience your extinction burst of anger and frustration as the tennis match in your head, between the old and new thoughts, plays match point and you reach the final result of who won.

You will uncover and unleash any remaining feelings and thoughts that have been festering in the pit of your body: those last deep-rooted fears that hold on as tight as they can in a desperate effort not to be thrown away.

Let it out and let it go.

Today may be a good day to have a pillow fight with the duvet, and, depending on how you best resolve things, it maybe a day to write those old beliefs and values an eviction notice out of your life.

However you are inspired to let go, make sure you open the box in your mind, that you have been avoiding exceptionally well up until now, and get rid of its contents. Let the new routine and thoughts have even more space to grow and flourish.

Today always reminds me of the moments in life when you're exhausted and you feel the darkness pushing in and you have nothing left to give to keep it at bay so you throw your hands up to the sky and shout for help.

Every day I see miracles and, from somewhere within, people they find their strength. They give it one last push and with that they let go and are free. The new thoughts and perceptions don't necessarily come rushing in but the relief of knowing that it could is profound.

Make sure you get some 'you time' today. Sit down and evict those last few old beliefs, values and perceptions and know that today is the day that they will no longer affect your future choices and decisions.

This is the last emotional detox day in this block of 40 days. You maybe physically groggy, mentally exhausted and emotionally lost. Just trust yourself and your goal/dream that this will only be for a day, and you need to let it play out.

If your routine and responsibilities permit, lay down and rest, put your comfy PJs on and allow your body the time it needs to heal.

Phoenix, take flight

Shelter me under your wings from the blazing fire

Let the darkness surround me

Become my blanket of protection

As part of me dies

Let the love from your fiery feathers

Give me courage and hope

As you guide me to great heights let this flicker of a flame in my heart turn into a raging fire

Let me emerge from underneath your wings

With strength, beauty and freedom

As I jump and take flight

31 DAY THIRTY

Harvest time, receiving great things for the changes you have made

CONGRATULATIONS!!!!

What a turn of events! You made it through the next set of rapids and you are now here at day 30. Today holds such a wonderful gift for you as you begin to see and receive the rewards of all your efforts.

However, it is all well and good being given a gift but how many of us are able to receive it? For some reason there seems to be a human condition of denying ourselves the very things that bring us happiness.

How many times have you seen or experienced this situation? Someone is really grateful for what you have done, so they buy you a gift and hand it over to you. Then there is a moment of apprehension from the receiver and maybe a conversation begins 'oh no, you don't need to do that, no you keep it', 'no, you have it' and so on.

After some resistance and reluctance the person accepts it. Why do we do this? Not only are you resisting and saying 'no, I can't receive any rewards for being myself and helping others' but you are also denying the gift giver their own happiness of being able to say thank you.

Instead, the conversation could go a little like this: 'thank you for such a wonderful gift, I really appreciate it'. Then you are happy because your actions have been recognised for how great they are and the other person is happy because they were able to show their appreciation. It's a win-win situation.

One way of looking at today is that you have spent all winter researching what seeds are best to plant on your land and you spent spring getting the land ready and planting the seeds. Then you protect them against the crows as they grow over the summer months. Harvest time arrives and you just sit staring at all the things you have grown. Along comes winter and you watch your harvest die away. You sit bewildered at why you haven't got anything and you struggle through the next winter.

It is a skill to slow down for a moment and have the self-worth and self-love that you deserve to receive the rewards for your efforts and enjoy them. There is no shame or guilt needed for you to say 'I have worked hard at changing my thoughts and my routine and now I get to enjoy the rewards of my efforts'.

Without realising it you have already begun to develop this skill through your accomplishments page, recognising what you have received for your efforts. So take out your notebook again and turn to the accomplishments page. Add any ways you have been rewarded for the effort you have put into changing.

Move through the day and be a receiver. Reaffirm to yourself that you receive all the great things every day of your life. Make a mental note how wonderful it is to receive something, especially when it is linked to your goal or dream.

32 DAY THIRTY ONE

Seeing your new habits as part of your life

One good day will now be building on top of another as you make your way through each moment of today. Today you will begin to see that, without much effort, your habit and new routine is now easy to carry out and has just become part of your life. This transition from the beginning of a place of discomfort and unsettlement to a place of ease and peace is so wonderful.

Did you get up this morning and, without much thought, carry out your tasks, find some happy thoughts or find some information that supported your new desires?

Can you recognise how you have changed your default setting? And all it took was to practise some new thoughts for long enough and go through an emotional and mental detox. Providing yourself with enough new experiences that supported your new beliefs and values enabled you to believe in your goal/dream becoming your reality.

With nine days left you will continue to make this default setting even easier to reach, even If at times you feel totally disconnected from your goal or dream. It won't take much effort to get back to this place of knowing and, most of all, be able to listen to and believe in yourself.

As we discussed earlier, adversity brings focus to the direction we are choosing to follow. What you will see and experience today is that by being optimistic and seeing the positives around you, you are continuing the conversation about how life is moving forward in the direction you wish it to go.

You are having your first experience of being a 'deliberate creator' and taking charge of the aspects of life you have control over, like your attitude and thoughts. Once you have reached the end of your 40 days and your goal/dream, you will have shown yourself just how easy it can be to accomplish things if you set up the routine for success.

Take out your notebook and top up your strengths and accomplishments pages. By now your writing will probably be very small by trying to squeeze it into the remaining tiny gaps. Before you started this journey have you ever spent this much time recognising what you are good at and all the things you have achieved? Have you achieved this much before in such a short space of time?

It's such a wonderful feeling to be in a place where you begin to dream and allow your dreams to not be limited by anything, even if those around you think you are a little weird for being so ambitious and optimistic. You know inside that you have already proved that things can be accomplished and come true, so why not again and again?

33 DAY THIRTY TWO

Seeing your confidence grow in taking new opportunities

Wow! Who is this confident go-getting person staring back at you in the mirror? You are demonstrating time and time again your new found confidence to take opportunities and go with them. However, this doesn't mean to say they don't still make you nervous or uneasy.

But you are getting better and more accomplished at moving from a place of fear to a place of courage, and maybe even acceptance of 'this is just how things work out best for me, otherwise life is too comfy and I won't continue to move forward'.

As you move through today, become aware of how different your actions and choices are. How many opportunities did you utilise? How many were mistakes? How many moved you closer to your goal or dream? Were the opportunities a conversation with another person or a sign by the road you passed? How much more aware are you of your surroundings?

How much more aware are you of yourself, and your quirks and traits? How much are you beginning to fall in love with yourself again? If you had recorded a day of thoughts you had 32 days ago and then again today, how differently would the two conversations look?

You are creating and attracting these new opportunities and the reason why they feel and look great is because you are spending most of your days hovering around the emotional level of: a) accepting–things not always going perfectly, b) love– for your transforming self, and sometimes c) joy–from receiving these new experiences.

Spend today just making a note of one day's worth of opportunities. They don't necessarily have to be opportunities you have taken, they can just be ones with potential, an opportunity you see but aren't interested in taking or going in the direction of, as well as ones you have taken.

Then this evening when you have written all the opportunities one day holds, write next to them why you spotted that opportunity. How is it linked to your goal or dream? You may even have to put 'I don't know yet why that would be linked to my goal or dream, maybe it was linked to the emotional level I was feeling'.

Then put a star next to all the opportunities that you had the confidence to pursue today, even if you surprised yourself with how you handled a situation or spoke up when normally you would sit quiet. Then put a tick next to opportunities that you could see yourself taking in the near future as your new thoughts and beliefs begin to become even more dominant.

One final assertion: it is always good to recognise the progress that has been made as it helps to keep up your level of motivation; as the saying goes, sometimes you can't see the wood for the trees. So take a step back. Are there any opportunities that you have completely surprised yourself with that you would have never gone for on day 1?

Can you see how much you have transformed?

> Everyday has the potential to be perfect.

34 DAY THIRTY THREE

Finding peace and serenity in your new way of thinking

When I speak of serenity and peace this doesn't mean that you are staying at one place on the emotional scale. If you do you will lose the variety of life and all the incredible experiences that come with the variety.

It means there is one aspect missing and I don't know if you have noticed its absence yet: the absence of worry. If you look back over the last few days, maybe over the last week, do you notice how you have been worrying less or maybe not even worrying at all, yet you are still making progress and moving forward?

The absence of worry means that you will have been acting and thinking with more clarity. Your actions aren't based on avoiding what you fear most but on what you desire.

That is one of the greatest rewards a person can receive and boy are you receiving it in large quantities. Can you see how you didn't need that worrisome part of you, that it was just a creation of your imagination, paralysing you with fear and stopping you from changing?

There will still be things to tick off on your to do and accomplishments list, but you are not procrastinating about it, instead you are making a plan about how it will be achieved. Who knows, you may even have decided which aspect of your to do list you want to set as you goal or dream to achieve on your next 40 day experience.

Imagine sitting down with your future self with a cup of tea and having a conversation with the future you, telling yourself how in just one year you have managed to carry out nine 40 day processes and have reached all nine goals. You will be able to share with others how transformed your life is and describe how different your reality looks.

Do you see how much potential one year holds? How much potential your life holds?

Today in your notebook I want you to imagine you are receiving a letter from your future self.

Write in the notebook what that letter would contain. Would it have words of reassurance or of elation at what your life now contains? The letter might talk about love, material things or the fact that you are calmer, look different, have more confidence, possess clarity on life and have a purpose.

Let the words flood onto the page. Let go and allow your imagination to flourish and dream. When you are done, reread what you have written. Do you wonder that if this was true how amazing it would be? There is no reason why this can't be true. Someone may not have done it before, but that doesn't mean it can't be done. There always needs to be a first time for everything.

Pin the letter somewhere where you will be able to see it regularly. Let it be a daily post-it note and a reminder of what life is becoming, of what each day is building towards, and how that journey will be free from worry and replaced with desire.

> The happier I am
>
> The richer I become
>
> In more ways than one

35 DAY THIRTY FOUR

Allowing yourself to dream and let go

What is a dream?

Is it just something we create with our imagination? Is it something that is unattainable? Is it a picture of being in a better place than you are now? Take out your notebook and write down your definition of a dream. The definition of a dream for me is the continuous focus on something that you desire to have or experience.

From this perspective no dream is unattainable. The only way for a dream not to be achieved is to stop trying. You may stop trying because you have set a certain timeframe for achieving it. If you don't succeed in that certain amount of time you may give up and maybe even think it is impossible.

If you allow yourself dream time everyday and slip into a day dream, you are letting go of the limitations that society and other people's beliefs have instilled in you. In turn, you set your own limitations and start believing in them. When you are day dreaming you are allowing yourself to be the creator of your experience and your actions push the expansion of mankind.

Once you practise going to this place of endless possibilities and come back to reality, look around you and the experiences you have had today. Are there any remaining memories or beliefs that you are still following and still practising everyday that actually no longer have a place in your life?

Are there any myths or other stories you believed in that actually, after all that you have learned over the last 34 days, aren't true? It may have been that it was your belief in them that made them true.

I believe that allowing your mind to wander and daydream is one of the most under-utilised parts of the brain. It was most utilised during the industrial revolution and quantum leaping truly did occur. However, because of the repetitive nature of the work that was created in that time we became conditioned not to dream. As society continues to evolve the inability to dream is becoming more apparent again with the age of technology.

As we have discussed before, greatness lies in a single action. Having a dream to be great, whether it is being a parent, boss or carrying out your job with integrity and pride, is just as noble as someone finding a cure for a disease for example.

So don't underestimate yourself or your dreams. You may not realise the greatness that lies within that one act and how much you as a person are needed for the rest of society to keep functioning and thriving.

Take a moment today to dream, to play out a scenario in your mind about how you wish today to progress. Allow yourself to receive the happiness that the daydream brings.

36 DAY THIRTY FIVE

Inspiring others through what you have discovered

Your story could be an inspiration to those around you. Your actions and teachings could then be the motivation for that person and be a catalyst for change.

I don't want to be morbid but let's fast forward to the moment they lay you in the ground or spread your ashes. Unlike the Egyptians, in modern times we generally don't bury a person with their belongings so all those material possessions that you have collected may be passed onto family members or distributed amongst the community.

The items may be forgotten about over time, however, there is something that won't be lost that will be passed from person to person and generation to generation. That is your story and your life's journey. What you achieved on a day to day basis maybe the missing piece of the jigsaw that your great-grandson needs to follow his desires, or pursue and believe in his dreams.

It is so fascinating to observe how everyone's story has an impact on someone else at some point. It maybe a marriage lasting for 60+ years, the job you did since you were 16 or an adventure you went on. Stories are told around the camp fire, sung in songs, written in books or shared around a collection of photographs.

It's not until you start to share your story that you realise how many people are inspired by it, find it motivating or discover some relief from seeing how you had moments of both adversity and celebration.

I always say our story is our legacy so you might as well make it a good one.

Look back over your life and the story you have created. I'm sure there have been times of adversity, triumph, clarity, fear and, of course, celebration. How many lessons have you learned? How many mistakes have you made?

The story you're thinking of right now will continue and inspire generations to come. It may not necessarily be through family members– it may be through friends or a stranger who discovers a diary or a message in a bottle.

Take the opportunity today to share your story, both the good and the bad, with someone or a group of people. Allow the lessons you've learned to help teach others. Allow people around you to celebrate your triumphs and find gratitude in your mistakes. Don't underestimate the power your words have and the impact they may have on another person's life.

It maybe 20 years from now that the very person you shared your story with will be sharing their story and saying how life changed the day they met you.

> Let my words
>
> Soothe your soul
>
> Open your heart
>
> And set you free

37 DAY THIRTY SIX

Clearing out the old to make room for the new

Open your eyes and take a look around your environment. What do you see? Is it immaculate, are you surrounded by sentimental objects or are you swamped by unfinished projects?

People underestimate how much their living space affects their life, but to clear it is not as easy as some may think. There is often much deliberation about whether you will one day need the item or whether you should keep it 'just in case'. A lot of clutter is there from a lack of focus and from the fear that what you have is not enough.

Your environment affects how much clutter and fog you have in your head. Letting go of things that were once a part of your identity is like

letting go of your old beliefs in a physical rather

than mental way.

Write down in your notebook who it is you want to be. Do you want to hold a specific job title or relationship status? Do you want your living space to look a certain way? Get some bin liners as you will definitely be needing them today. Pick one room you want to start in. Pick up an item and ask yourself if it fits into any of the categories describing who you want to be that you have just written down. If it is of great sentimental value you can have a memory box for it to live in or keep it out on display.

If it is a project you were thinking of doing, ask yourself honestly are you really interested in doing that project? Or because of all the changes you have made do you have new projects that you want to accomplish instead? Does that object fit into the new project? If the answer is no then it's time to let it go. You have not failed just because you didn't end up using it in the end, your dreams have just changed and the experience of completing that project no longer inspires you.

As you are sorting through things, make sure you wipe down that area. It may seem a bit obvious but you will understand once you have completed that room. When you have filled a bag with things you no longer need, put it outside. Don't leave it by the door or tucked in a corner as it will end up being left there. If you put it outside your house then it has definitely transitioned out of your life and you can begin to see your environment transforming.

It will also help you to stop becoming overwhelmed, as you will see and feel the results of all your efforts. This might be something you do over time, one room a day. Just make sure you make it through the whole space. Also when you are going through your house and you finish one room, reward yourself. Make a cup of tea and sit in the room for a moment to enjoy what you have achieved: the space, peace and clarity.

This is one of the most emotional and mental detoxing activities that you can do and you may need to go through the process a few times (such as every time you carry out a 40 day process) to reach the kind of space you desire.

You will be surprised by how being surrounded by things that only support the projects you are interested in right now helps you to identify with the person you are becoming and you will find it easier expressing that part of you each day. Also you have now created room in your life for new things to arrive. As I have described previously, you can't take hold of tomorrow's opportunities if you are still holding onto yesterday's experiences.

38 DAY THIRTY SEVEN

Falling in love with your new qualities

When you wake up this morning and open your eyes and see your new environment, you will really start to see how your life is shaping up to look like that you have been dreaming of.

As you move to the bathroom and see yourself in the mirror, who do you see? Are you beginning to see the person you have described in your strengths and accomplishments pages? Now would be a good time to take up your notebook again and write down any new strengths as well as the accomplishments you made yesterday.

When we don't see our inner truth regularly, that pure part of ourselves, we aren't allowing that part of us to grow. I always think happiness is the best look a person can have. By allowing ourselves to love all of who we are, we are, without realising it, allowing others to see and love that part of us too.

Building on day 16 and the love you began to discover for yourself, are you able to see that self-love comes from within? It's not up to anyone else to give – it's up to you. I'm sure you will still see things that may need a little work but try to see the things that you have already worked on and changed.

People still get surprised when the mirroring effect occurs, as you start to recognise, allow and love a new part of yourself. You'll see how many other people begin to see it too. As you move through the day, listen to how people are speaking to you. Are they talking about a topic that is linked to your goal or dream? Are they speaking about your accomplishments or the strengths you have written down in your notebook?

Loving yourself and who you are is another fantastic skill to have and this is another skill the strengths and accomplishment pages have provided you with. You may look in the mirror and decide it's time for your physical appearance to catch up with your new way of thinking. You might get a haircut, buy a new item of clothing, get your ears pierced or whatever you feel inspired to do.

Allow your image and your physical body to begin to reflect the new you and how you are feeling. Don't worry if you turn a few heads. It's time for you to shine, enjoy the banter and know deep inside that it doesn't matter what people say about you. There is, and always will be, someone who will be with you and love you unconditionally.

That person is you.

So go through today and every time you catch yourself in a reflection, mirror or just have a thought about yourself, make sure you always include a loving thought. It might be 'I really love the person I am', 'I am beautiful' or 'I have so many good qualities that help those around me'. Start to change the conversation you have with yourself to one of love.

Are you starting to see the skills you keep practising?

> Let go – of past experiences influencing future choices
>
> Let love –accepting and loving who you are including your uniqueness
>
> And dream –dream big allowing yourself to create an incredible future

39 DAY THIRTY EIGHT

A day of reflection

As you are nearing the end of the 40 days, take a moment today to rest. Continue to carryout your routine but don't do anything else today as the last few days have been full of changes to your physical environment and physical appearance.

Like I covered on day 30, allow yourself to bask. Admire and receive your harvest, acknowledge all those small achievements that you have made that have led up to this point.

Enjoy how, in just 38 days, your life has started to gather momentum in the new direction you are taking. Reflect on all the times you went up and down the emotional scale such as the times when you thought you were getting nowhere, the times which were difficult as you let go of something and the times when you received or took an opportunity that inspired every inch of you.

When we take time out of the equation, do you see how, in just a moment of your life compared to all those years before, you have turned things around? Can you see how you have moved away from a place of disempowerment where you felt helpless and thought things were never going to change? You are now in a position of empowerment as you have taken control of how you are feeling and thinking at the same time as having some incredible experiences.

Now is the time to let the whole process sink deep into your core. If you have achieved what you set out to achieve, fantastic! If you are not quite there yet you still have two days left and a lot can happen in 48 hours.

If you have set a big dream to accomplish and aren't quite there yet, do you see how this 40 day process has helped to sort out something that needed completing first in order to be able to move on and obtain that dream? Can you see what it is you need to do over the next 40 days to move up another level and be one step closer to your big dream?

I can't emphasise enough that it is not the huge changes you make that create a better life, but those changes you make each day. Those single drips add up and suddenly you have a lake. It's these small changes, even a change in how you see certain situations, that really have a large impact on life and how you are building on solid foundations as you continue to build your better life.

If, whilst you have been reflecting, you remember any more strengths and accomplishments, don't forget to add them to your notebook. Sit back and admire what you have done and achieved as it's nothing short of a miracle.

And that miracle is you.

If our life was like the sea

The rhythm never changes as the waves and days come and go

There are days of raging storms and destruction

Then there are days of stillness and serenity

The sea sparkles with beauty, as thousands of diamonds shine as they dance on the surface of the water

There are no limitations when living in the sea

Something can be as big or small as it wants to be

But everything has its own part to play and place in this life.

40 DAY THIRTY NINE

Celebrate good times, come on!

Time to get the champagne flowing and the party poppers out. Wow, what a gift to receive today, did you get it yet? Have you achieved what you wanted to achieve?

I am getting excited even at the thought of it! Celebrate, be joyful, bounce and jump around the room if you want to. If you are not celebrating your goal/dream being fully achieved, celebrate what it is that you have received so far over the last 39 days.

Rejoice in the fact that you are here, alive and awake – that is definitely something to celebrate! Celebrate the fact that you have a whole 24 hours to have fun and treats for yourself.

If you haven't gathered what the theme is today, I will take the opportunity to spell it out for you: C.E.L.E.B.R.A.T.E! There is always something to celebrate each and everyday, we just need to find it and when we do, turn loose, and allow the excitement and happiness to be what fills every cell, every thought, and every action of our day.

Why wait until your birthday to celebrate that you are part of this world? It is definitely something worth celebrating everyday! By now you will have received something enormous or be very close to achieving your goal or dream. It may take a couple more days but it feels only moments away.

The routine you started 39 days ago is nothing out of the ordinary. It is just a part of who you are and a part of your life. You may even be at the stage where it wouldn't matter if you continued to carry it out every day, it's so well integrated into the new part of you that it will always have a place in your life.

You may even have enjoyed getting to this point so much that you have started to plan what it is that you wish to achieve next and what the next 40 days will be dedicated to.

Oooh I'm so excited just writing these words and thinking about the unlimited potential life has for you. Now you know that it will take a little effort, some emotional and mental detoxing, but you'll get there and reach it.

Get yourself a present today, but not just any gift. It should be something that symbolizes the fact that you can create and receive anything you want to in this life if you set your mind to it. You can practise the thoughts and take the opportunities that will get you there, knowing that every 40 days will move you one step closer.

Share your achievements with a friend who can also celebrate what you have achieved.

Red flag! Today is not the day to forget to do the routine. Remember that if you miss a day you have to start again. Make sure you keep finding the time to do your routine today and tomorrow.

41 DAY FORTY

What a journey!

What a journey you have been on, what an incredible last 40 days. First of all, I am so proud of you. Proud that you have persevered and persisted in getting this far.

Not everyone makes it and the very fact that you are reading this page means that you have shown strength, courage, integrity, honour, belief and so much more. You will receive that which you have asked for because you have put the effort in to get there. The amount of effort you have put in will be the amount you will receive.

From this place I hope you begin to realise that this is just the first step of many transformations you will go through. You may continue to build on what you have achieved over the last 40 days for a while, or you may head in a completely new direction. It is your right to choose.

Over the last 40 days you have explored the concept of what it truly means to not only dream but to pursue your dreams. It is a concept that I hope millions of people around the world will continue to do until the end of time.

By following your dreams and taking steps to achieve them, each day has blazed a trail for others to follow in your footsteps. You are being a role model to those around you, maybe your family, friends, colleagues or someone you speak to on the bus.

Not only have you found your dreams and gone after them, you have also discovered and got to know a very important person in your life.

You.

That person sometimes gets forgotten about on a day to day basis, with people and life asking different things of you. But you have made time for yourself for the last 40 days; let that continue as it's so important to take time to fill up your own cup.

So may this be the first step of many towards the life you dream of experiencing. May life's adversity come and go, leaving its lessons from which we can grow from, knowing our thoughts are the key to our experiences and transforming our life. I hope you set time aside each day to celebrate the moments filled with laughter and love.

42 CONCLUSION

When carrying out a transformation many things occur and, as you have seen, these changes can occur in a short space of time. Changing your life doesn't need to be hard, strenuous or painful. It doesn't need to consume your whole life. It begins with just one action that is carried out daily to become more aligned with where you want to be.

As you sit back and look over the last 40 days and enjoy receiving your goal/dream, or being one step closer, let this be a lasting memory of how simple it can be to change your life, to move to the next level and have new experiences.

The 40 day process is about bringing focus into your life and into each day. There are so many distractions every day and some I believe we are not even aware of. There are so many different pieces of information that our brains are having to process, sort through or discard. You're working harder than you think and, as technology speeds everything up, we are managing to fit more activities into 24 hours than we have ever done before.

This can mean that we are so busy trying to keep up with everything each day that we forget to plan for tomorrow. I am not talking about planning your responsibilities but rather planning your happiness. How many times in your life have you organised something that brings you happiness? For most individuals it's only about once a year when they go on holiday.

Why can't every day contain one thing that makes us smile? Why do we have to wait until we go on holiday, then fit as much as we can into 7-14 days? There is a tendency to come back home and then start looking forward to next year because you have to wait until you next go away to feel relaxed, relieved and peaceful.

Going away on holiday is just one example to help you crank up the cogs in your mind that you don't have to wait to feel happiness. There will be at least one moment a day that has the potential to put a smile on your face and fill your body up with good feelings.

What you have shown over the last 40 days is self-discipline, a quality that people don't very easily identify with. Over the past 40 days you have had the self-discipline to work towards your goal or dream. As you may have discovered, self-discipline can push you out of your comfort zone from time to time. However, you will always receive something worthwhile by doing it.

Let this new skill go at the top of your achievements page –that you have the self-discipline to achieve anything you want to! The question is what is it that you want? For me, when I first carried out this process, I set a really ambitious dream and by the end of the 40 days I hadn't accomplished it. I had accomplished something else instead that I had totally forgotten about needed doing. But the incredible thing is that to reach that big dream I needed to have accomplished this other thing first.

As I keep carrying out my 40 days I am still heading towards that initial goal/ dream, but I find the 40 days are moving me up level by level to where I need to be to receive the initial goal/dream. Move at the pace with which you feel most comfortable. For me it was too much of a leap to go from the place I was at to the place of receiving that goal/dream so I have broken it down into smaller stepping stones. This may be how you work best or you may be a person where you are able to carry out a 360 degree turn in life. Be proud and celebrate the way you best achieve your goal or dreams as what works for you has lots to offer and teach the rest of us.

So when you are planning your next 40 days, here are some things to consider. Have you had a good enough experience that the process works? Are you able to dream bigger this time? If you were like me and had a big dream, do you know what it is you need to achieve next to bring you one step closer to getting there? Have at least one day off between your sets of 40 days, just to give yourself chance to become acquainted with this new level of life and what it brings.

Did you notice how each day brought its own set of emotions and how you didn't just stay at one level on the emotional scale? Instead, you moved up and down, but overall heading in the general direction of up. Our emotions give our days variety. I think even the happiest people in the world have a negative thought once in a while, they just have the tools to turn things around a bit quicker and let go or solve what it was that is bothering them. They are able to do it quickly because they have spent many hours practising the same things that you have over the last 40 days. They remind themselves of their strengths and accomplishments and keep up their level of motivation by knowing that they deserve to feel happy and in love with life and themselves.

It's important to take a moment to look at the butterfly effect that you have experienced. The changes that have occurred over the last few weeks will continue to yield results over the next few weeks as there is a delay between changing your thoughts and receiving those changes in reality. As you continue the sets of 40 days they will begin to build one on top of another and gather momentum. If you think a tidal wave starts with a single wave and the power of one wave combines with another and another to create a surge of power. Just like a tidal wave begins with an earthquake under the sea, adversity does the same in our life. It is a catalyst for us to ask for something different and provides us with enough motivation to start moving in a new direction.

There is a reason why the saying 'steps to success' is used so regularly. It is what it takes to have sustainable happiness and dreams. Taking one step at a time means that you are never going to stop moving towards your goals. So if you get the urge when you're halfway towards your goal/dream to stop and turn back, just remember day 20. Instead of turning back and going the same distance but in the direction of where you came from, continue to walk that distance but in the direction you want to go.

Over the last 40 days you have been practising:

Letting go: of past influences influencing future choices.

Allowing love: falling in love with the wonderful person you are everyday.

Dreaming big: focusing on your dreams and knowing they will come true.

I am going to leave you with my definition of 'hope' and my wish is for your days to continue to be filled with hope, happiness and love.

HOPE:

Is to wish for and welcome something,

with the expectation of its fulfilment with confidence and belief.

It is to desire something,

with little reason or justification,

by cherishing and trusting the aspiration of good.

Dear Reader,

I had such a wonderful time writing this book and exploring transforming your life in 40 days.

I would love to hear what you thought about this book.

1. If you go to Amazon

2. Type Naomi Sharp into the search box and press enter

3. Click on the book

4. Scroll down until you reach the star chart

5. Click the button 'write a review'

With gratitude,

Naomi Sharp

43 OTHER BOOKS BY NAOMI

A Diary Of Dreams

Finding love and happiness by living your dreams following the death of a family member. Hugh watched his mom Ally's happiness dissolve away as her depression took hold as all she could see was a new absence in her life of a love that was no longer there. Hugh dreamed of his mom finding her happiness, falling in love and rediscovering the magic of life, and allowing love that once was to transform as they embark on a new chapter in life. Hugh decided to create a map of dreams as a vision board of all the thing he wanted to happen in his life. This resulted in an adventure that took him and Ally to meet the people they needed to meet, the places they needed to go and the dreams they desired to experience on the road to discovering how truly magical life is. This book helps inspire you to plan and dream the life you're desiring, empowering women and children to have the courage to follow their heart's desires, and enabling their ambitions in life to flourish. An incredible story of how family, dreams and love can help you achieve anything you want.

Living Life With The Glass Half Full

An inspiring true story of how a young girl chooses to learn from life's adversity with the help of horses. She travels to Ireland, France and America to understand how to live a better, happier life, and to understand what it truly means to heal. The story follows her from her younger days causing mischief in nursery through to the frustration of being dyslexic in school. This leads up to her whole world being turned around with a profound realisation. All the while different horses are guiding her path through the years with their constant friendship and companionship, highlighting some of the facts of life Naomi has picked up along the way. The book includes a bonus feature for your own personal development providing ways for you to analyse your life's problems and turn them into positives with surprising ease. It encourages you to work through your own challenges by changing your perceptions on how you view life and adversity so that you are able to change your life. This book provides a true account of how, by changing your own perceptions of life and looking for the lessons to be learned in the adversity, the adventure of life becomes more about using those lessons to help your dreams to become your reality rather than allowing the adversity to become your future.

ABOUT THE AUTHOR

www.naomisharpauthor.com

Naomi began making notes when she was 10 years old, always having a notebook ready to jot down the next profound thought or idea. As Naomi grew older her writing began to develop even though through her teenage years the English language wasn't something she loved as she found it difficult to put into words what she was thinking. By the time Naomi reached university she spent time around people who helped her to understand how to turn her thoughts into words on the page, and gave her the tools so Naomi could write what she was thinking and feeling.

It was like the flood gates had opened, and Naomi began to each day write things down in her notebook. But it wasn't until 6 years on that Naomi would write her first book Living Life With The Glass Half Full, where she would be able to share her story of changing life's adversity into lessons learnt. No sooner had she finished that book she was onto her next, as she became inspired to write A Diary Of Dreams, her first fiction. Naomi describes the experience as "downloading a story, like a movie was playing in front of me and I was writing down what was happening moment by moment".

Naomi continues to write as her passion grows to inspire people to heal and find happiness and hope in their life. She feels story telling is an incredible way to pass on wisdom and life's truths.

Naomi Sharp trained as an Occupational Therapist but became fascinated in how horses help people to heal not only physically but also mentally and emotionally. Her passion for understanding how we can help our bodies to heal and our dreams to become reality has brought some breath-taking experiences into her life, as well as the opportunity to meet some incredible people and places.

Naomi Sharp

Made in the USA
Charleston, SC
19 November 2015